Sharing the Beauty of China 中华优秀传统文化传承发展工程支持项目

汉英对照 Chinese-English

毛泽东诗词与诗意画
ILLUSTRATED POEMS OF MAO ZEDONG

Translated by Xu Yuanchong

许渊冲 译

CHINA INTERCONTINENTAL PRESS

图书在版编目（CIP）数据

毛泽东诗词与诗意画：汉英对照 / 毛泽东著；许渊冲译. -- 北京：五洲传播出版社，2020.1
（中华之美）
ISBN 978-7-5085-4341-3

Ⅰ．①毛… Ⅱ．①毛… ②许… Ⅲ．①毛主席诗词－选集－汉、英②毛泽东（1893-1976）－法书③中国画－作品集－中国－现代 Ⅳ．① A841.4 ② A841.5

中国版本图书馆 CIP 数据核字（2019）第 273553 号

"中华之美"丛书

主　　编　陈陆军
出 版 人　荆孝敏

毛泽东诗词与诗意画（汉英对照）

译　　者　许渊冲
责任编辑　王　峰
助理编辑　秦慧敏
版式设计　殷金花
制　　版　北京紫航文化艺术有限公司
出版发行　五洲传播出版社
地　　址　北京市海淀区北三环中路 31 号生产力大楼 B 座 6 层
邮　　编　100088
发行电话　010-82005927，010-82007837
网　　址　http://www.cicc.org.cn，http://www.thatsbooks.com
印　　刷　深圳市彩美印刷有限公司
版　　次　2020 年 1 月第 1 版第 1 次印刷
开　　本　155mm×230mm　　1/16
印　　张　12.25
字　　数　155 千
定　　价　146.00 元

共享中华之美
——"中华之美"丛书序

"文化是一个国家、一个民族的灵魂。"要了解中国,自然也离不开中国文化。中华民族五千多年文明历史所孕育的中华优秀传统文化,积淀了丰富多样的、弥足珍贵的民族精神财富,古典诗词是其中的瑰宝。

中国在历史上是一个"诗歌的国度",每个历史年代都留下了丰硕的诗歌成果,其中不少名篇名句,脍炙人口,传诵至今。中国古典诗词以其精炼优美的语言、丰富真挚的情感、含蓄委婉的意境,传唱千古而不衰,滋养着世代中国人的心灵。它们传递着中国人独特的思想智慧和艺术审美内涵,承载着中华民族的精神追求、人文价值和生命力量,是中华传统文化的精髓。

"中华之美"丛书选取的这些作品,是三千年来有代表性的中国优秀诗篇。中国古典诗词注重抒情、写景,善于表现各种复杂细微的情感。古代诗词中的优秀之作往往写得富于形象性和音乐性。我曾经提出,翻译是"美化之艺术",提出译作要追求意美、音美、形美"三美"。通过优秀的译作,将这些中华优秀诗作介绍给世界上更广大的读者,是我的心愿。

中国古典诗词善于表现自然之美及人与自然的融合。诗和画号称姊妹艺术,所以中国古人常说"诗中有画,画中有诗"。"中华之美"丛书精选了各个历史时代的中国经典画作,与诗词作品及相关历史背景有机结合起来,体现形神兼备、情景交融的中华美学追求。

英国诗人艾略特说过:"个人的才智有限,文化的力量无穷。"21世纪是全球化的世纪。新世纪的新人不但应该了解全球的文化,而且应该使本国文化走向世界,成为全球文化的一部分,使世界文化更加灿烂辉煌。

近年来,中国古典诗词热在海内外不断升温,不仅激发了中国人对中华传统文化的热爱之情,也在许多海外人士尤其海外青少年心里埋下了中国文化的种子。衷心希望"中华之美"丛书能够帮助更多海外读者增进对中国文化的了解,让读者在审美过程中获得愉悦、感受中华文化魅力,使读者对中华文化"知之,好之,乐之",共享中华之美。

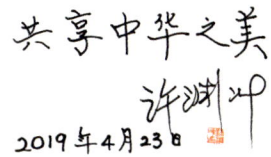

共享中华之美
许渊冲
2019年4月23日

PREFACE TO THE *SHARING THE BEAUTY OF CHINA* SERIES

Xu Yuanchong

"Culture is the soul of a country and its people." To better understand China, it is only natural to want to know more about the diverse and rich Chinese culture accumulated in a history of more than 5,000 years. Reading and enjoying classical poetry of China is indeed one of the shortcuts in this regard as well as a great joy for many.

Historically, China was a "country of poetry". Every historical period has left beautiful poems, many of which are well-known and continue to be recited so far. Chinese classical poetry, known for its refined and beautiful language, is concise but cherishes an implicit and euphemistic mood, striking a responsive chord among Chinese. These poems show their ideological wisdom, cultural pursuits and humanistic values.

Classical poems form an unbroken line considered to be the cream of poetry created in the past 3,000 years. All of them pay high attention to lyricism and scenery, expressing various complex and subtle emotions. Since classical Chinese poetry represent the combination of beauty in sense, sound and form, anyone seeking to translate them needs to try to reproduce the "three beauties" of the original. It is my wish to see a vivid materialization of this theory in doing translation work, because I strongly believe this theory has profound historical and cultural foundations.

Chinese classical poetry is good at expressing the beauty of nature and the integration of human emotions and nature. In the eyes of the Chinese, poetry and painting are close companions in the art world, so they often say, "There are 'paintings' in poetry, and there are 'poems' in paintings." The *Sharing the Beauty of China* series selects the best of the Chinese classical paintings created in various historical periods, combined with poems and related historical background in an organic way, that embody the pursuit of Chinese aestheticism with both form and spirit and the blending of scenes.

Thomas Steams Eliot (1888-1965), the English poet, once said that individual intelligence is limited, but culture is infinite. In the 21st Century which is believed to be a century of globalization, people should not only understand global culture, but also make sure their own culture is made available to the world, thus becoming a part of the global culture, and adding luster to the world culture.

Recent years have seen increasing popularity of Chinese classical poetry at home and abroad. This not only stimulates the Chinese people's love for their traditional culture, but also buries the seeds of Chinese culture in the hearts of many overseas people. I sincerely hope the *Sharing the Beauty of China* series can help more overseas readers of all age groups to gain pleasure and feel the charm of Chinese culture in the aesthetic process, enabling them to know and enjoy Chinese culture.

April 23, 2019

(Translated by Guozhen Wang)

目录
CONTENTS

五古·挽易昌陶 ——————————— 001

七古·送纵宇一郎东行 ——————— 006

虞美人 枕上 ——————————————— 011

贺新郎 别友 ——————————————— 013

沁园春 长沙 ——————————————— 017

菩萨蛮 黄鹤楼 ————————————— 023

西江月 秋收起义 ———————————— 024

西江月 井冈山 ————————————— 027

清平乐 蒋桂战争 ———————————— 028

采桑子 重阳 —————————————— 030

如梦令 元旦 —————————————— 033

减字木兰花 广昌路上 ————————— 035

蝶恋花 从汀州向长沙 ————————— 038

Five-Character-Ancient-Verse
Elegy on Yi Changtao ——————————————————— 002

Seven-Character-Ancient-Verse
Seeing Luo Zhanglong Off to Japan ———————————— 008

Tune: The Beautiful Lady Yu
Written on My Pillow ——————————————————— 011

Tune: Congratulations to the Bridegroom
To Yang Kaihui ————————————————————— 013

Tune: Spring in a Pleasure Garden
Changsha ————————————————————————— 017

Tune: Buddhist Dancers
Yellow Crane Tower ——————————————————— 023

Tune: The Moon over the West River
The Autumn Harvest Uprising ——————————————— 024

Tune: The Moon over the West River
Mount Jinggang ————————————————————— 027

Tune: Pure Serene Music
The Warlords Fight ———————————————————— 029

Tune: Picking Mulberries
The Double Ninth ————————————————————— 030

Tune: Like a Dream
New Year's Day —————————————————————— 033

Tune: Shortened Form of Magnolia
On the Guangchang Road ————————————————— 035

Tune: Butterflies Lingering over Flowers
March from Tingzhou to Changsha —————————————— 038

渔家傲 反第一次大"围剿"	040
渔家傲 反第二次大"围剿"	043
菩萨蛮 大柏地	044
清平乐 会昌	048
十六字令三首	051
忆秦娥 娄山关	054
六言诗·给彭德怀同志	058
七 律·长征	060
念奴娇 昆仑	062
清平乐 六盘山	069
沁园春 雪	070
临江仙 给丁玲同志	077
五 律·挽戴安澜将军	078
五 律·张冠道中	081
五 律·喜闻捷报	084
七 律·人民解放军占领南京	087
七 律·和柳亚子先生	089

Tune: Pride of Fishermen
Against the First "Encirclement" Campaign ——————— 040

Tune: Pride of Fishermen
Against the Second "Encirclement" Campaign ——————— 043

Tune: Buddhist Dancers
Place of Big Cypress ——————————————————— 044

Tune: Pure Serene Music
Huichang ——————————————————————— 048

Three Poems of Sixteen Words ——————————— 053

Tune: Dream of a Maid of Honor
The Pass of Mount Lou ——————————————— 054

Six-Character-Verse
General Peng Dehuai ——————————————— 058

Seven-Character-Regular-Verse
The Long March ———————————————————— 061

Tune: Charm of a Maiden Singer
Mount Kunlun ——————————————————— 064

Tune: Pure Serene Music
Spiral Mountain ——————————————————— 069

Tune: Spring in a Pleasure Garden
Snow ———————————————————————— 070

Tune: Immortal at the River
To Ding Ling ——————————————————— 077

Five-Character-Regular-Verse
Elegy on General Dai Anlan ——————————— 078

Five-Character-Regular-Verse
After Leaving Yan'an ——————————————— 081

Five-Character-Regular-Verse
Rejoicing over the Victory ——————————— 085

Seven-Character-Regular-Verse
Capture of Nanjing by the People's Liberation Army ——— 087

Seven-Character-Regular-Verse
Reply to Mr. Liu Yazi ——————————————— 089

浣溪沙 和柳亚子先生	093
浣溪沙 和柳亚子先生	095
浪淘沙 北戴河	096
七律·和周世钊同志	099
五律·看山	100
七绝·莫干山	102
七绝·五云山	105
水调歌头 游泳	107
蝶恋花 答李淑一	112
七绝·观潮	116
七律二首·送瘟神	119
七绝·刘蕡	122
七律·到韶山	125
七律·登庐山	126
七绝·为女民兵题照	129
七绝·屈原	131
七绝二首·纪念鲁迅八十寿辰	132

Tune: Sand of Silk-Washing Stream
Reply to Mr. Liu Yazi ———————————————— 093

Tune: Sand of Silk-Washing Stream
Reply to Mr. Liu Yazi ———————————————— 095

Tune: Ripples Sifting Sand
The Seaside—Beidaihe ——————————————— 096

Seven-Character-Regular-Verse
In Reply to Comrade Zhou Shizhao ——————————— 099

Five-Character-Regular-Verse
Mountain Views ————————————————— 101

Seven-Character-Quatrain
Mount Mogan ——————————————————— 102

Seven-Character-Quatrain
The Rainbow Cloud Mountain———————————— 105

Tune: Prelude to the Melody of Water
Swimming ———————————————————— 108

Tune: Butterflies Lingering over Flowers
The Immortals—Reply to Li Shuyi ————————— 112

Seven-Character-Quatrain
Watching the Tidal Bore ——————————————— 116

Two Poems of Seven-Character-Regular-Verse
Get Away, Pest! —————————————————— 120

Seven-Character-Quatrain
Liu Fen ——————————————————————— 123

Seven-Character-Regular-Verse
Shaoshan Revisited———————————————— 125

Seven-Character-Regular-Verse
Up Mount Lu ——————————————————— 126

Seven-Character-Quatrain
Militia Women—Inscription on a Photo ——————— 129

Seven-Character-Quatrain
Qu Yuan —————————————————————— 131

Two Poems of Seven-Character-Quatrain
On the 80th Anniversary of Lu Xun's Birthday——————— 132

七律·答友人 —————————— 134

七绝·为李进同志题所摄庐山仙人洞照 ———— 137

七律·和郭沫若同志 —————————— 138

卜算子 咏梅 ———————————————— 141

七律·冬云 ————————————————— 142

满江红 和郭沫若同志 —————————— 144

杂言诗·八连颂 ——————————————— 148

七律·吊罗荣桓同志 ————————————— 152

贺新郎 读史 ———————————————— 155

念奴娇 井冈山 ——————————————— 158

水调歌头 重上井冈山 ———————————— 162

念奴娇 鸟儿问答 —————————————— 166

七律·洪都 ————————————————— 172

七律·有所思 ———————————————— 174

七绝·贾谊 ————————————————— 177

七律·咏贾谊 ———————————————— 178

Seven-Character-Regular-Verse
Reply to a Friend —————————————————— 134

Seven-Character-Quatrain
The Immortal's Cave —————————————————— 137

Seven-Character-Regular-Verse
Reply to Comrade Guo Moruo ———————————— 138

Tune: Song of Divination
Ode to the Mume Blossom ————————————— 141

Seven-Character-Regular-Verse
Winter Clouds —————————————————————— 142

Tune: The River All Red
Reply to Comrade Guo Moruo ———————————— 145

Ode to the Eighth Company ———————————————— 148

Seven-Character-Regular-Verse
Elegy on Comrade Luo Ronghuan——————————— 152

Tune: Congratulations to the Bridegroom
Reading History———————————————————— 155

Tune: Charm of a Maiden Singer
Mount Jinggang———————————————————— 158

Tune: Prelude to the Melody of Water
Mount Jinggang Reascended——————————————— 162

Tune: Charm of a Maiden Singer
Dialogue between Two Birds ————————————— 166

Seven-Character-Regular-Verse
Nanchang, Capital of Jiangxi ——————————————— 172

Seven-Character-Regular-Verse
Yearning ————————————————————————— 174

Seven-Character-Quatrain
Jia Yi ———————————————————————————— 177

Seven-Character-Regular-Verse
On Jia Yi ————————————————————————— 179

雨中登峨眉金刚坡下寄傅抱石成都归来记之 抱石

听泉图（局部） 现代 傅抱石
Listening to the Spring (partial), Contemporary, Fu Baoshi

五古·挽易昌陶

1915年5月

去去思君深，思君君不来。愁杀芳年友，悲叹有余哀。
衡阳雁声彻，湘滨春溜回。感物念所欢，踯躅南城隈。

城隈草萋萋，涔泪侵双题。采采余孤景，日落衡云西。
方期沆瀁游，零落匪所思。永诀从今始，午夜惊鸣鸡。

鸣鸡一声唱，汗漫东皋上。冉冉望君来，握手珠眶涨。
关山蹇骥足，飞飙拂灵帐。我怀郁如焚，放歌倚列嶂。

列嶂青且茜，愿言试长剑。东海有岛夷，北山尽仇怨。
荡涤谁氏子，安得辞浮贱。子期竟早亡，牙琴从此绝。

琴绝最伤情，朱华春不荣。后来有千日，谁与共平生？
望灵荐杯酒，惨淡看铭旌。惆怅中何寄，江天水一泓。

Five-Character-Ancient-Verse
Elegy on Yi Changtao
May 1915

Farther away, the deeper I think of you,
However deep, you will not come in view,
Your death grieves me, your friend of younger days;
However long I sigh, my grief still stays.
The Southern Peak is sad with wild geese's song;
By lakeside grievous water flows along.
Can I not at this sight the past recall?
I loiter long by southern city wall.

By city wall the dewy grasses grow
Like bitter tears along my cheeks which flow.
I'm left alone 'mid grass with colored cloud;
The sun is setting west of mountains proud.
When I did hope we would go far and wide.
Who could foretell you'd wither like grass dried?
From now on I cannot see you again;
Cock's crow at midnight would thrill me with pain.

竹林七贤图 现代 傅抱石
Seven Sages of the Bamboo Grove, Contemporary, Fu Baoshi

高士罢琴图 现代 傅抱石
The Hermit Stops Playing the Instrument, Contemporary, Fu Baoshi

The cock's first crow reminds me of my friend;
I stroll to the east without aim or end.
I fondly wish you'd come with bygone years;
I wring my hands, my eyes brimful of tears.
Steep mountains hinder a galloping steed;
The whirlwind stirs your funeral screen with speed.
My heart in flame, my grief can't be oppressed;
I roar a song, leaning on mountain crest.

The mountain crest is crimson-red and green;
I would fain try my long sword with edge keen.
In Eastern Ocean there're barbarians;
On Northern Mountains stand tartarians.
Who would be sons so mean or slaves so base
As not to purify their country's face?
But the good lutist died an early death.
How could the broken lute breathe pleasing breath?

The broken lute would break my strong heart-string;
Your rosy face won't bloom again in spring.
Afterwards e'en though there's so many a day,
Who'll go together with me the same way?
Before your coffin I pour a cup of wine,
Gazing on your funeral board, I pine.
Where can I confide my sad thoughts? I sigh
To see deep water under deep blue sky.

七古·送纵宇一郎东行

1918 年 4 月

云开衡岳积阴止,天马凤凰春树里。
年少峥嵘屈贾才,山川奇气曾钟此。
君行吾为发浩歌,鲲鹏击浪从兹始。
洞庭湘水涨连天,艨艟巨舰直东指。
无端散出一天愁,幸被东风吹万里。
丈夫何事足萦怀,要将宇宙看秭米。
沧海横流安足虑,世事纷纭从君理。
管却自家身与心,胸中日月常新美。
名世于今五百年,诸公碌碌皆余子。
平浪宫前友谊多,崇明对马衣带水。
东瀛濯剑有书还,我返自崖君去矣。

初春 现代 傅抱石
Early Spring, Contemporary, Fu Baoshi

SEVEN-CHARACTER-ANCIENT-VERSE
SEEING LUO ZHANGLONG OFF TO JAPAN
April 1918

Clouds break o'er Southern Mountains and deep gloom's dispelled;
Peaks amid vernal trees look like phoenix and horse.
While young, like Qu and Jia in talent you excelled;
Mountains and streams inspire you with tremendous force.
You're going and I'm singing stirring songs for you;
The giant roc will beat the waves from now and here.
The lake and river stretching skyward out of view;
Your steamer like a warship to the east will steer.
My sorrow for no reason overspreads the sky;
Luckily the east wind blows it to the far-off land.
For nothing burdening his mind a man should sigh
But see the world as if it were a grain of sand.
Don't worry about counter-currents in the sea
And pay no heed to world events in sorry plight.
Take care your body and your soul be pure and free;
And sun and moon e'er shed on your mind a new light.
High fame will last not longer than five hundred years;
The mediocre cannot boast that they are great.
Before Waves-Calming Palace friendly smile appears;
A strip of water severs our land from their strait.
I leave the seaside cliff when I see you no more.
Write to me when you wash your sword by
Eastern Shore!

烟雨迷蒙图 现代 傅抱石
Misty Drizzle, Contemporary, Fu Baoshi

仕女 现代 傅抱石
A Maiden, Contemporary, Fu Baoshi

虞美人 枕上

1921 年

堆来枕上愁何状,江海翻波浪。
夜长天色总难明,寂寞披衣起坐数寒星。

晓来百念都灰尽,剩有离人影。
一钩残月向西流,对此不抛眼泪也无由。

TUNE: THE BEAUTIFUL LADY YU
WRITTEN ON MY PILLOW

1921

Like what would sorrow look, piled on my pillows?
A sea of surging billows.
As night is long and dawn is slow to come from far,
Lonely I rise in nightgown to count star on star.

When morning comes, all thoughts fade from my mind.
How can I leave you far behind?
A hooklike waning moon floats in the western spheres.
At sight of this, can I refrain from shedding tears?

A Willow in Spring Breeze, Contemporary, Fu Baoshi

贺新郎 别友

1923 年

挥手从兹去。更那堪凄然相向，苦情重诉。

眼角眉梢都似恨，热泪欲零还住。

知误会前番书语。

过眼滔滔云共雾，算人间知己吾和汝。

人有病，天知否？

今朝霜重东门路，照横塘半天残月，凄清如许。

汽笛一声肠已断，从此天涯孤旅。

凭割断愁丝恨缕。

要似昆仑崩绝壁，又恰像台风扫寰宇。

重比翼，和云翥。

TUNE: CONGRATULATIONS TO THE BRIDEGROOM
TO YANG KAIHUI

1923

Waving my hand, I part from you.

How can I bear to face you sad and drear,

Telling me your sorrows anew?

Keeping back a warm dropping tear,

月落乌啼霜满天 现代 傅抱石
Crows Cry at Moonset across a Frosty Sky, Contemporary, Fu Baoshi

Your eyes and brows reveal,
The bitter grief you feel.
The misunderstanding arose from what I wrote,
But it will melt like clouds that fleet and mists that float.
In the human world, who
Knows me better than you?
Does heaven know
Man's weal and woe?

The road of Eastern Gate with morning frost is white.
The waning moon halfway up the sky sheds her light
So sad and drear
On the Pool Clear.
The whistle shrills and broken is my heart.
From now on, we'll be lonely, far apart.
Of sorrow let's cut off the string,
Of grief let us break through the ring,
Just as Mount Kunlun thrusts its cliffs asunder
Or the typhoon sweeps the world under.
Then like two birds we'll fly
And cleave the clouds on high.

毛泽东《沁园春·长沙》词意图（一） 现代 傅抱石
Artistic Conception of Mao Zedong's Changsha in the Tune "Spring in a Pleasure Garden" (I), Contemporary, Fu Baoshi

沁园春 长沙

1925 年

独立寒秋，湘江北去，橘子洲头。

看万山红遍，层林尽染；漫江碧透，百舸争流。

鹰击长空，鱼翔浅底，万类霜天竞自由。

怅寥廓，问苍茫大地，谁主沉浮？

携来百侣曾游。忆往昔峥嵘岁月稠。

恰同学少年，风华正茂；书生意气，挥斥方遒。

指点江山，激扬文字，粪土当年万户候。

曾记否，到中流击水，浪遏飞舟？

TUNE: SPRING IN A PLEASURE GARDEN
CHANGSHA

1925

In autumn cold alone stand I,

Of Orange Islet at the head,

Where River Xiang northward goes by.

I see hill on hill all in red

And wood on wood in a deep dye,

The river green down to the bed,

毛泽东《沁园春·长沙》词意图（二，局部）
Artistic Conception of Mao Zedong's Changsha in the Tune "Spring in a Pleasure Garden" (II, partial)

In speed a hundred barges vie.
Far and wide eagles cleave the blue;
Up and down fish in shallows glide:
All creatures strive for freedom under frosty skies.
Lost in immensity, I wonder who,
Upon this boundless earth, decide
All beings' fall and rise.

With many friends I oft came here.
How thick with salient days the bygone times appear!
When, students in the flower of our age,
Our spirit bright was at its height,
Full of the scholar's noble rage,
We criticized with all our might.
Pointing to stream and hill,
Writing in blame or praise,
We treat'd like dirt all mighty lords of olden days.
Do you remember still,
Swimming mid-stream, we struck waves to impede
That boats which passed at flying speed?

毛泽东《沁园春·长沙》词意图（三）
Artistic Conception of Mao Zedong's Changsha in the Tune "Spring in a Pleasure Garden" (III)

毛泽东《菩萨蛮·黄鹤楼》词意图 现代 傅抱石

Artistic Conception of Mao Zedong's Yellow Crane Tower in the Tune "Buddhist Dancers", Contemporary, Fu Baoshi

菩萨蛮 黄鹤楼

1927 年春

茫茫九派流中国，沉沉一线穿南北。
烟雨莽苍苍，龟蛇锁大江。

黄鹤知何去？剩有游人处。
把酒酹滔滔，心潮逐浪高！

TUNE: BUDDHIST DANCERS
YELLOW CRANE TOWER
Spring 1927

Wide, wide through the land flow nine streams full to the brim;
Long, long from south to north threads one line deep and dim.
Shrouded in grizzling mist and drizzling rain,
Tortoise and Snake hold the River in chain.

Where is the yellow crane in flight,
Leaving for visitors a site?
I pledge with wine the endless flood;
With rolling waves upsurges my blood.

西江月 秋收起义

1927 年

军叫工农革命,旗号镰刀斧头。
匡庐一带不停留,要向潇湘直进。

地主重重压迫,农民个个同仇。
秋收时节暮云愁,霹雳一声暴动。

TUNE: THE MOON OVER THE WEST RIVER
THE AUTUMN HARVEST UPRISING
1927

Our Army rose for proletarian revolution;
A hammer and a sickle mark our banners red.
From the Lu Mountains we marched with resolution;
To Rivers Xiao and Xiang we fought our way ahead.

The landlords piling up oppressions thick and high;
The peasants bearing common hatred one and all.
The evensing clouds look heavy in the autumn sky,
The revolt breaks out as a thunderbolt does fall.

毛泽东词意图（局部） 现代 傅抱石
Artistic Conception of Mao Zedong's Poem (partial), Contemporary, Fu Baoshi

毛泽东《西江月·井冈山》词意图 现代 傅抱石

Artistic Conception of Mao Zedong's Mount Jinggang in the Tune "The Moon over The West River", Contemporary, Fu Baoshi

西江月 井冈山

1928 年秋

山下旌旗在望，山头鼓角相闻。
敌军围困万千重，我自岿然不动。

早已森严壁垒，更加众志成城。
黄洋界上炮声隆，报道敌军宵遁。

TUNE: THE MOON OVER THE WEST RIVER
MOUNT JINGGANG

Autumn 1928

Flags and banners in sight below,
Drum-beats mingle atop with bugle-blast.
Surrounded ring on ring by the foe,
Aloft we still stand fast.

Our ranks as firm as rock,
Our wills form a new wall.
The cannon roared at Huangyang Block,
The foe fled at night-fall.

蜀江图 现代 傅抱石

A River of Sichuan, Contemporary, Fu Baoshi

清平乐 蒋桂战争

1929 年秋

风云突变,军阀重开战。

洒向人间都是怨,一枕黄粱再现。

红旗跃过汀江,直下龙岩上杭。

收拾金瓯一片,分田分地真忙。

Tune: Pure Serene Music
The Warlords Fight
Autumn 1929

A sudden burst of wind and rain:
The warlords fight again.
Sowing on earth but grief and pain,
They dream of reigning but in vain.

O'er River Ting our red flags leap;
To Longyan and Shanghang we sweep.
A part of golden globe in hand,
We're busy sharing out the land.

毛泽东《采桑子·重阳》词意图（局部） 现代 傅抱石
Artistic Conception of Mao Zedong's The Double Ninth in the Tune
"Picking Mulberries" (partial), Contemporary, Fu Baoshi

采桑子 重阳

1929 年 10 月

人生易老天难老，岁岁重阳。
今又重阳，战地黄花分外香。

一年一度秋风劲，不似春光。
胜似春光，寥廓江天万里霜。

TUNE: PICKING MULBERRIES
THE DOUBLE NINTH

October 1929

Nature does not grow old as fast as man;
Each year the Double Ninth comes round.
And now the Double Ninth comes round.
How sweet are yellow flowers on the battleground!

See autumn reign with heavy winds once every year,
Unlike springtime.
Far more sublime,
The boundless sky and waters blend with endless rime.

毛泽东《如梦令·元旦》词意图（局部） 现代 傅抱石
Artistic Conception of Mao Zedong's New Year's Day in the Tune "Like a Dream" (partial), Contemporary, Fu Baoshi

如梦令 元旦

1930 年 1 月

宁化、清流、归化，路隘林深苔滑。

今日向何方，直指武夷山下。

山下山下，风展红旗如画。

TUNE: LIKE A DREAM
NEW YEAR'S DAY

January 1930

Ninghua, Qingliu, Guihua:
Deep forests, slippery moss and narrow paths.
Where are we bound today?
Straight below. Mount Wuyi we go our way.
Below,
Below,
The wind unrolls
Red flags like scrolls.

漫天飞雪炫双眸 现代 傅抱石
White Snow Dazzles Eyes, Contemporary, Fu Baoshi

减字木兰花 广昌路上

1930 年 2 月

漫天皆白,雪里行军情更迫。
头上高山,风卷红旗过大关。

此行何去?赣江风雪迷漫处。
命令昨颁,十万工农下吉安。

TUNE: SHORTENED FORM OF MAGNOLIA
ON THE GUANGCHANG ROAD

February 1930

The sky all white,

The army march in snow, the more eager to fight.

O'erhead loom crags;

We go through the strong pass with wind- frozen red flags.

Where are we hurrying?

Towards the River Gan where snow is flurrying.

Orders out yesterday:

One hundred thousand troops to Ji'an make their way.

漫天飞雪炫双眸（局部）
White Snow Dazzles Eyes (partial)

平沙落雁图（局部） 现代 傅抱石
Wild Geese over the Sands (partial), Contemporary, Fu Baoshi

蝶恋花 从汀州向长沙

1930 年 7 月

六月天兵征腐恶，万丈长缨要把鲲鹏缚。
赣水那边红一角，偏师借重黄公略。

百万工农齐踊跃，席卷江西直捣湘和鄂。
国际悲歌歌一曲，狂飙为我从天落。

TUNE: BUTTERFLIES LINGERING OVER FLOWERS
MARCH FROM TINGZHOU TO CHANGSHA

July 1930

Heavenly troops wage war in June on evil lords,
Ready to capture rocs and whales with long, long cords.
Beyond the River Gan a corner blazes red,
Thanks to the army with Huang Gonglue at its head.

A million workers and peasants all leap and bound,
Sweeping Jiangxi, on Hunan and Hubei they pound.
The stirring strains of "the Internationale" rise;
A furious storm comes down for our sake from the skies.

渔家傲 反第一次大"围剿"

1931年春

万木霜天红烂漫，天兵怒气冲霄汉。
雾满龙冈千嶂暗，齐声唤，前头捉了张辉瓒。

二十万军重入赣，风烟滚滚来天半。
唤起工农千百万，同心干，不周山下红旗乱。

Tune: Pride of Fishermen
Against the First "Encirclement" Campaign

Spring 1931

Under a frosty sky all woods in gorgeous red,
The wrath of godlike warriors strikes the sky overhead.
Mist shrouds Longgang and dims the thousand peaks about.
All voices shout:
"Ah! Zhang Huizan is captured by our men ahead!"

Two hundred thousand troops invade Jiangxi again,
Raising a cloud of dust sky-high like hurricane.
Arouse a million workers and serfs to take the gun,
United as one,
How wild below Mount Pillar our red flags will run!

毛泽东《渔家傲·反第一次大"围剿"》词意图（局部） 现代 傅抱石
Artistic Conception of Mao Zedong's Against The First "Encirclement" Campaign in the Tune "Pride Of Fishermen" (partial), Contemporary, Fu Baoshi

毛泽东诗意图（局部） 现代 傅抱石
Artistic Conception of Mao Zedong's Poem (partial), Contemporary, Fu Baoshi

渔家傲 反第二次大"围剿"

1931 年夏

白云山头云欲立，白云山下呼声急，枯木朽株齐努力。
枪林逼，飞将军自重霄入。

七百里驱十五日，赣水苍茫闽山碧，横扫千军如卷席。
有人泣，为营步步嗟何及！

TUNE: PRIDE OF FISHERMEN
AGAINST THE SECOND "ENCIRCLEMENT" CAMPAIGN

Summer 1931

Atop the White Cloud Mountain the clouds seem to rear;
Below the White Cloud Mountain cry the foes for fear.
Withered thees and rotten wood try hard to come near,
A forest of rifles appear,
But our flying army falls on them from the sphere.

We've marched seven hundred li in days fifteen
From brimming River Gan to Wuyi Mountains green.
A thousand foes are swept away as a mat clean.
Someone bewails unseen:
On forts built at each step, alas! he could not lean.

菩萨蛮 大柏地

1933 年夏

赤橙黄绿青蓝紫,谁持彩练当空舞?
雨后复斜阳,关山阵阵苍。

当年鏖战急,弹洞前村壁。
装点此关山,今朝更好看。

TUNE: BUDDHIST DANCERS
PLACE OF BIG CYPRESS

Summer 1933

Red, orange, yellow, green, blue, indigo, violet
Who's dancing with a colored band in the sky fire-lit?
After the rain the sinking sun is seen;
The mountain pass exhales floods of deep green.

A furious battle raged then on this spot;
The village walls are still riddled with shot.
Dotted today with these traces of war,
The mountain pass looks fairer than before.

毛泽东《菩萨蛮·大柏地》词意图 现代 傅抱石
Artistic Conception of Mao Zedong's Place of Big Cypress in the Tune "Buddhist Dancers",
Contemporary, Fu Baoshi

毛泽东《菩萨蛮·大柏地》词意图（局部）
Artistic Conception of Mao Zedong's Place of Big Cypress in the Tune "Buddhist Dancers" (partial)

清平乐 会昌

1934 年夏

东方欲晓,莫道君行早。
踏遍青山人未老,风景这边独好。

会昌城外高峰,颠连直接东溟。
战士指看南粤,更加郁郁葱葱。

TUNE: PURE SERENE MUSIC
HUICHANG

Summer 1934

Dawn tinges the eastern skies.
Boast not you start before sunrise.
We have trodden green mountains without growing old.
What scenery unique here we behold!

Peaks after peaks outside Huichang, as if in motion,
Undulate until they join with the eastern ocean.
Our warriors, pointing south, see Guangdong loom
In a richer green and lusher gloom.

毛泽东《清平乐·会昌》词意图 现代 傅抱石
Artistic Conception of Mao Zedong's Huichang in the Tune "Pure Serene Music", Contemporary, Fu Baoshi

毛泽东《十六字令·山》词意图（局部） 现代 傅抱石
Artistic Conception of Mao Zedong's Poems of Sixteen Words on Peaks (partial), Contemporary, Fu Baoshi

十六字令三首

1934 — 1935 年

其一
山，快马加鞭未下鞍。
惊回首，
离天三尺三。

其二
山，倒海翻江卷巨澜。
奔腾急，
万马战犹酣。

其三
山，刺破青天锷未残。
天欲堕，
赖以拄其间。

毛泽东《十六字令·山》词意图（局部）
Artistic Conception of Mao Zedong's Poems Of Sixteen Words on Peaks (partial)

THREE POEMS OF SIXTEEN WORDS
1934–1935

I
Peaks!
Whipping the steed without dismounting, I
Look back surprised
To be three-foot-three off the sky.

II
Peaks,
Turbulent sea with monstrous breakers white,
Or galloping steeds
In the heat of the fight.

III
Peaks
Piercing the blue without blunting the blade,
The sky would fall
But for this colonnade.

毛泽东词意－苍山如海（局部） 现代 傅抱石
Artistic Conception of Mao Zedong's Line "Green Mountains like the Tide" (partial), Contemporary, Fu Baoshi

忆秦娥 娄山关

1935 年 2 月

西风烈，长空雁叫霜晨月。
霜晨月，马蹄声碎，喇叭声咽。

雄关漫道真如铁，而今迈步从头越。
从头越，苍山如海，残阳如血。

TUNE: DREAM OF A MAID OF HONOR
THE PASS OF MOUNT LOU

February 1935

The wild west wind blows strong;
The morning moon shivers at the wild geese's song.
On frosty morn
Steeds trot with hooves outworn
And bugles blow forlorn.

Fear not the strong pass iron-clad on all sides!
The summit's now surmounted with big strides.
Surmounted with big strides,
Green mountains like the tide;
The sunken sun blood-dyed.

毛泽东《忆秦娥·娄山关》词意图（局部） 现代 傅抱石

Artistic Conception of Mao Zedong's The Pass of Mount Lou in the Tune "Dream of a Maid of Honor" (partial), Contemporary, Fu Baoshi

雄关漫道真如铁,而今迈步从头越。从头越,苍山如海,残阳如血。毛主席忆秦娥词意 辛巳 抱石写

蜀江图（局部） 现代 傅抱石
A River of Sichuan (partial), Contemporary, Fu Baoshi

六言诗·给彭德怀同志

1935 年 10 月

山高路远坑深，
大军纵横驰奔。
谁敢横刀立马？
唯我彭大将军！

SIX-CHARACTER-VERSE
GENERAL PENG DEHUAI

October 1935

From east to west by bounds and leaps our army sweeps.
All the way over mountains steep and trenches deep.
Who is there wielding his sword and rearing his horse?
It is none but General Peng of our mighty force.

更喜岷山千里雪（局部） 现代 傅抱石

Glad to See the Min Range Snow-clad for Miles and Miles (partial), Contemporary, Fu Baoshi

七律·长征

1935 年 10 月

红军不怕远征难，万水千山只等闲。
五岭逶迤腾细浪，乌蒙磅礴走泥丸。
金沙水拍云崖暖，大渡桥横铁索寒。
更喜岷山千里雪，三军过后尽开颜。

Seven-Character-Regular-Verse
The Long March
October 1935

Of the trying long march the Red Army makes light:
Thousands of rivers and mountains are barriers slight.
The five serpentine Ridges outspread like rippling rills;
The pompous Wumeng peaks tower but like mole-hills.
Against warm cloudy cliffs beat waves of Golden Sand;
With cold iron-chain Bridge River Dadu is spanned.
Glad to see the Min Range snow-clad for miles and miles,
Our warriors who have crossed it break into broad smiles.

念奴娇 昆仑

1935 年 10 月

横空出世,莽昆仑,阅尽人间春色。
飞起玉龙三百万,搅得周天寒彻。
夏日消溶,江河横溢,人或为鱼鳖。
千秋功罪,谁人曾与评说?

而今我谓昆仑:
不要这高,不要这多雪。
安得倚天抽宝剑,把汝裁为三截?
一截遗欧,一截赠美,一截还东国。
太平世界,环球同此凉热。

策杖行旅图（局部） 现代 傅抱石
Trekking with a Cane (partial), Contemporary, Fu Baoshi

试张季仁墨作山水图 现代 傅抱石
Imitation of Zhang Jiren's Inkwash Landscape, Contemporary, Fu Baoshi

TUNE: CHARM OF A MAIDEN SINGER
MOUNT KUNLUN

October 1935

Above the earth, across the blue,

Monster Kunlun in white,

You have feasted your eye on the world's fairest view.

Like three million white jade dragons in flight,

You have chilled the sky through.

When summer melts your snow

And rivers overflow,

For fish and turtles men would become food.

But who has ever judged if you

Have done for ages more ill than good?

Kunlun, I tell you now:

You need not be so high,

Nor need you so much snow.

Could I but lean against the sky

And draw my sword to cut you into three!

I would give to Europe your crest

And to America your breast

And leave in the Orient the rest.

In a peaceful world young and old

Might share alike your warmth and cold!

试张季仁墨作山水图（局部）
Imitation of Zhang Jiren's Inkwash Landscape (partial)

江山如此多娇 现代 傅抱石 关山月
Our Motherland Is So Rich in Beauty, Contemporary, Fu Baoshi and Guan Shanyue

毛泽东《清平乐·六盘山》词意图（局部） 现代 傅抱石
Artistic Conception of Mao Zedong's Spiral Mountain in the Tune "Pure Serene Music" (partial), Contemporary, Fu Baoshi

清平乐 六盘山

1935 年 10 月

天高云淡，望断南飞雁。
不到长城非好汉，屈指行程二万。

六盘山上高峰，红旗漫卷西风。
今日长缨在手，何时缚住苍龙？

TUNE: PURE SERENE MUSIC
SPIRAL MOUNTAIN

October 1935

The sky is high, the clouds are light,
The wild geese flying south are out of sight.
We are not heroes unless we reach the Great Wall;
Counting up, we've done twenty thousand li in all.

Of Spiral Mountain at the crest,
Red flags wave in wanton winds from the west.
With the long cord in hand today,
When shall we bind the Dragon Gray?

沁园春 雪

1936 年 2 月

北国风光，千里冰封，万里雪飘。

望长城内外，惟余莽莽；大河上下，顿失滔滔。

山舞银蛇，原驰蜡象，欲与天公试比高。

须晴日，看红装素裹，分外妖娆。

江山如此多娇，引无数英雄竞折腰。

惜秦皇汉武，略输文采；唐宗宋祖，稍逊风骚。

一代天骄，成吉思汗，只识弯弓射大雕。

俱往矣，数风流人物，还看今朝。

TUNE: SPRING IN A PLEASURE GARDEN
SNOW

February 1936

See what the northern countries show:

Hundreds of leagues ice-bound go;

Thousands of leagues flies snow.

毛泽东《沁园春·雪》词意图 现代 傅抱石
Artistic Conception of Mao Zedong's Snow in the Tune "Spring in a Pleasure Garden",
Contemporary, Fu Baoshi

毛泽东《沁园春·雪》词意图（局部）
Artistic Conception of Mao Zedong's Snow in the Tune "Spring in a Pleasure Garden" (partial)

Behold! Within and without the Great Wall

The boundless land is clad in white,

And up and down the Yellow River, all

The endless waves are lost to sight.

Mountains like silver serpents dancing, Highlands like waxy elephants advancing,

All try to match the sky in height.

Wait till the day is fine

And see the fair bask in sparkling sunshine,

What an enchanting sight!

Our motherland so rich in beauty

Has made countless heroes vie to pay her their duty.

But alas! Qin Huang and Han Wu

In culture not well bred,

And Tang Zong and Song Zu

In letters not wide read.

And Genghis Khan, proud son of Heaven for a day,

Knew only shooting eagles by bending his bows.

They have all passed away;

Brilliant heroes are those

Whom we will see today!

韶山招待所（局部） 现代 傅抱石
Shaoshan Guest House (partial), Contemporary, Fu Baoshi

临江仙 给丁玲同志

1936 年 12 月

壁上红旗飘落照，西风漫卷孤城。
保安人物一时新。洞中开宴会，招待出牢人。

纤笔一枝谁与似？三千毛瑟精兵。
阵图开向陇山东。昨天文小姐，今日武将军。

TUNE: IMMORTAL AT THE RIVER
TO DING LING

December 1936

On streaming banners red, departing sunbeams fall,
The western wind is whirling round the city wall.
Your presence brightens all of us and brings high glee,
The cave is turned into a banquet hall
To welcome you, a prisoner set free.

Second to none, though delicate your pen appears,
Yet it may brave three thousand musketeers.
East of the mountains Long you go in proud array;
In yesterday's fair writer one reveres
Heroic captain of today.

五律·挽戴安澜将军

1943年3月

外侮需人御,将军赋采薇。
师称机械化,勇夺虎罴威。
浴血东瓜守,驱倭棠吉归。
沙场竟殒命,壮志也无违。

FIVE-CHARACTER-REGULAR-VERSE
ELEGY ON GENERAL DAI ANLAN

March 1943

We must repel the foreign foe;
Singing martial songs did you go.
Leading Division motorized,
The bears and tigers you despised.
At East Towns you waged bloody fight;
You drove the Japs with main and might.
You gave your life in battlefield,
Your will to serve the State fulfilled.

龙蟠虎踞今胜昔（局部） 现代 傅抱石
The Tiger Girt with Dragon Outshines Days Gone By (partial), Contemporary, Fu Baoshi

万竿烟雨图 现代 傅抱石
Bamboos in a Misty Rain, Contemporary, Fu Baoshi

五律·张冠道中

1947 年

朝雾弥琼宇，征马嘶北风。
露湿尘难染，霜笼鸦不惊。
戎衣犹铁甲，须眉等银冰。
踟蹰张冠道，恍若塞上行。

FIVE-CHARACTER-REGULAR-VERSE
AFTER LEAVING YAN'AN

1947

The morning mist veils the grey sky;
In northern wind my steed's neigh's lost.
Heavy with dew, no dust can fly;
No crow is startled in hoar frost.
My battledress like armor weighs;
My eyebrows look like silver white.
We came to and fro on our ways,
As if the frontier were in sight.

万竿烟雨图（局部）
Bamboos in a Misty Rain (partial)

五律·喜闻捷报

1947 年

秋风度河上,大野入苍穹。
佳令随人至,明月傍云生。
故里鸿音绝,妻儿信未通。
满宇频翘望,凯歌奏边城。

抢渡大渡河 现代 傅抱石
Rush to Cross the Dadu River, Contemporary, Fu Baoshi

FIVE-CHARACTER-REGULAR-VERSE
REJOICING OVER THE VICTORY
1947

The river swept by autumn breeze,
The vast plain extends to the sky.
The festival comes as we please:
The moon shines bright, the clouds float by.
No news is brought by the wild geese,
From my homeland and family.
I gaze up on high without cease:
The border town's loud with victory.

毛泽东《七律·人民解放军占领南京》诗意图（局部） 现代 傅抱石
Artistic Conception of Mao Zedong's Poem Capture of Nanjing by the People's Liberation Army (partial), Contemporary, Fu Baoshi

七 律·人民解放军占领南京

1949 年 4 月

钟山风雨起苍黄，百万雄师过大江。
虎踞龙盘今胜昔，天翻地覆慨而慷。
宜将剩勇追穷寇，不可沽名学霸王。
天若有情天亦老，人间正道是沧桑。

SEVEN-CHARACTER-REGULAR-VERSE
CAPTURE OF NANJING BY THE PEOPLE'S LIBERATION ARMY

April 1949

Over the Purple Mountains sweeps a storm headlong:
Our troops have crossed the great river, a million strong.
The Tiger girt with Dragon outshines days gone by;
Heaven and earth o'erturned, our spirits ne'er so high!
With our courage unspent pursue the foe o'erthrown!
Do not fish like the Herculean King for renown!
Heaven would have grown old were it moved to emotions;
The world goes on with changes in the fields and oceans.

今古输赢一笑间（局部） 现代 傅抱石
A Smile over Win and Loss (partial), Contemporary, Fu Baoshi

七律·和柳亚子先生

1949 年 4 月 29 日

饮茶粤海未能忘，索句渝州叶正黄。
三十一年还旧国，落花时节读华章。
牢骚太盛防肠断，风物长宜放眼量。
莫道昆明池水浅，观鱼胜过富春江。

SEVEN-CHARACTER-REGULAR-VERSE
REPLY TO MR. LIU YAZI

April 29, 1949

I cannot forget our tea-drinking at Canton,
Nor our verse exchanged 'neath yellow leaves in Chongqing.
After thirty-one years, back in the ancient town,
I read your fine verse 'mid falling blooms in late spring.
Do not grumble too much for fear your heart should break;
Try to take longer views in judging anything.
Do not complain too shallow is the Kunming Lake.
For watching fish, it's better than River Rich-Spring.

煮茶图 现代 傅抱石
Cooking Tea, Contemporary, Fu Baoshi

华岳松云图 现代 傅抱石

Clouds and Pines in the Huashan Mountain, Contemporary, Fu Baoshi

浣溪沙 和柳亚子先生

1950 年 10 月

长夜难明赤县天，
百年魔怪舞翩跹，
人民五亿不团圆。

一唱雄鸡天下白，
万方乐奏有于阗，
诗人兴会更无前。

Tune: Sand of Silk-Washing Stream
Reply to Mr. Liu Yazi

October 1950

Dawn came late to Crimson Land drowned in long, long night:
Demons and monsters danced for ages in great delight,
Five hundred million people yearned to reunite.

At the cock's clairon call the world sees broad daylight:
Music plays far and near, songs from Yutian come here,
Our poets' verve attains an unprecedented height.

虎溪三笑（局部） 现代 傅抱石
Three Hermits Laugh by the Huxi Stream (partial), Contemporary, Fu Baoshi

浣溪沙 和柳亚子先生

1950 年 11 月

颜斶齐王各命前，
多年矛盾廓无边，
而今一扫纪新元。

最喜诗人高唱至，
正和前线捷音联，
妙香山上战旗妍。

TUNE: SAND OF SILK-WASHING STREAM
REPLY TO MR. LIU YAZI

November 1950

The prince commanded and was commanded to obey;
This contradiction developed from day to day.
Now a new era dawns: the prince was swept away.

To our delight the poet chanting loud comes here,
And news of victory reaches us from the frontier.
How nice the fighting flags in Korea would appear!

浪淘沙 北戴河

1954 年夏

大雨落幽燕，白浪滔天，秦皇岛外打鱼船。
一片汪洋都不见，知向谁边？

往事越千年，魏武挥鞭，东临碣石有遗篇。
萧瑟秋风今又是，换了人间。

TUNE: RIPPLES SIFTING SAND
THE SEASIDE—BEIDAIHE

Summer 1954

On northern land a heavy rain is pouring,
Sky-high white waves are roaring.
Off Emperor's Isle the fishing boats outgoing
All lost to sight in the wide, wide sea foaming,
Who knows where they are roaming?

Over a thousand years ago by the seaside,
Whipping his steed, Wu of Wei took a ride.
Verses on his eastern trip to Mount Stone still remain.
The autumn wind is blowing now as bleak as then,
But changed is the world of men.

毛泽东《浪淘沙·北戴河》词意图（局部） 现代 傅抱石
Artistic Conception of Mao Zedong's The Seaside—Beidaihe in the Tune "Ripples Sifting Sand" (partial), Contemporary, Fu Baoshi

富春晓色（局部） 现代 傅抱石

The Morning View of Fuchun River (partial), Contemporary, Fu Baoshi

七律·和周世钊同志

1955年10月

春江浩荡暂徘徊，又踏层峰望眼开。
风起绿洲吹浪去，雨从青野上山来。
尊前谈笑人依旧，域外鸡虫事可哀。
莫叹韶华容易逝，卅年仍到赫曦台。

SEVEN-CHARACTER-REGULAR-VERSE
IN REPLY TO COMRADE ZHOU SHIZHAO

October 1955

In spring we loiter by the rolling river's side;
Again we reach the peaks with our eyes open wide.
The wind rises o'er islets green, 'mid waves it drops,
The rain from verdurous fields comes up to mountain tops.
Before wine-cups we talk and laugh still as of yore;
Trifling disputes abroad are but things to deplore.
Do not regret our golden hours of days gone by!
Thirty years passed, again we're on this Terrace high.

假日千山（局部） 现代 傅抱石
The Qianshan Range (partial), Contemporary, Fu Baoshi

五律·看山

1955 年

三上北高峰，杭州一望空。
飞凤亭边树，桃花岭上风。
热来寻扇子，冷去对佳人。
一片飘飖下，欢迎有晚鹰。

Five-Character-Regular-Verse
Mountain Views
1955

Thrice I ascend the Northern Height;
The city seems lost to my sight.
By Phoenix Pavilion trees tower;
The wind sweeps over Mount Peach Flower.
When it's hot, I seek the Fan Hill;
I face Peak Beauty when it's chill.
With wings like floating cloud so free,
At dusk Mount Eagle welcomes me.

假日千山（局部）
The Qianshan Range (partial)

七绝·莫干山

1955 年

翻身跃入七人房，
回首峰峦入莽苍。
四十八盘才走过，
风驰又已到钱塘。

SEVEN-CHARACTER-QUATRAIN
MOUNT MOGAN

1955

Re-entering the seven-seated carriage, I
Look back and find the peaks melt into the blue sky.
From the forty-eight twists and turns we've just come down,
My wind-driven car arrives at the lakeside town.

千山竞秀（局部）　现代　傅抱石
Gorgeous Mountains (partial), Contemporary, Fu Baoshi

七绝·五云山

1955 年

五云山上五云飞，
远接群峰近拂堤。
若问杭州何处好，
此中听得野莺啼。

SEVEN-CHARACTER-QUATRAIN
THE RAINBOW CLOUD MOUNTAIN

1955

Over the Rainbow Cloud Mountain rainbow clouds fly,
O'ershadow distant peaks and caress the lake nearby.
If you ask me where I would like to linger long,
It's here where I may listen to orioles' song.

毛泽东词意－神女应无恙（局部） 现代 傅抱石

Artistic Conception of Mao Zedong's Line "Mount Goddess Standing Still as Before" (partial), Contemporary, Fu Baoshi

水调歌头 游泳

1956 年 6 月

才饮长沙水，又食武昌鱼。
万里长江横渡，极目楚天舒。
不管风吹浪打，胜似闲庭信步，今日得宽余。
子在川上曰：逝者如斯夫！

风樯动，龟蛇静，起宏图。
一桥飞架南北，天堑变通途。
更立西江石壁，截断巫山云雨，高峡出平湖。
神女应无恙，当惊世界殊。

Tune: Prelude to the Melody of Water
Swimming
June 1956

Having relished a cup of Changsha water
And then a dish
Of Wuchang fish,
I swim across the thousand-mile long river,
And as far as can reach the eye,
I find the wide, wide Southern sky.
Braving wild winds and waves, I feel more pleasure
Than strolling in a yard at leisure:
What freedom I enjoy today!
The Master on a stream did say:
"Thus pass all things away!"

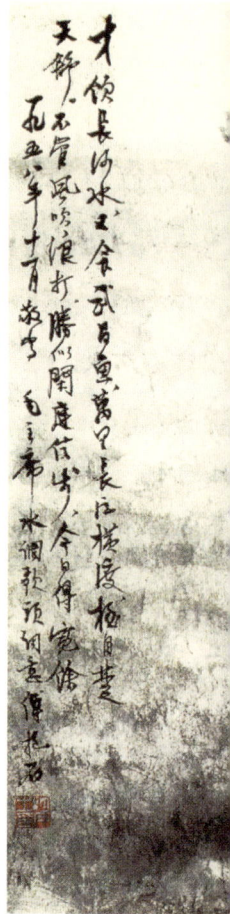

Sails in the wind go past,
Tortoise and Snake stand fast;
Great works are on the make:
A bridge will fly from north to south o'er there,
Turning the chasm into a thoroughfare.
Stone walls will stand across the river in the west
To hold back clouds and rains o'er Mount Witch's crest
Until between steep cliffs emerges a placid lake.
Mount Goddess standing still as before
Would feel surprised to find no more
The world of yore.

毛泽东《水调歌头·游泳》词意图（一） 现代 傅抱石

Artistic Conception of Mao Zedong's Swimming in the Tune "Prelude to the Melody of Water" (I), Contemporary, Fu Baoshi

毛泽东《水调歌头·游泳》词意图 (二)
Artistic Conception of Mao Zedong's Swimming in the Tune "Prelude to the Melody of Water" (II)

毛泽东《蝶恋花·答李淑一》词意图 现代 傅抱石

Artistic Conception of Mao Zedong's The Immortals—Reply to Li Shuyi in the Tune "Butterflies Lingering over Flowers", Contemporary, Fu Baoshi

蝶恋花 答李淑一

1957 年 5 月 11 日

我失骄杨君失柳,杨柳轻飏直上重霄九。
问讯吴刚何所有,吴刚捧出桂花酒。

寂寞嫦娥舒广袖,万里长空且为忠魂舞。
忽报人间曾伏虎,泪飞顿作倾盆雨。

TUNE: BUTTERFLIES LINGERING OVER FLOWERS
THE IMMORTALS—REPLY TO LI SHUYI

May 11, 1957

You've lost your Willow and I've lost my Poplar proud,
Their souls ascend the highest heaven, light as cloud.
The Woodman, asked what he has for wine,
Brings out a nectar of laurels divine.

The lonely Goddess of the Moon, large sleeves outspread,
Dances up endless skies for these immortal dead.
From the earth comes the news of the Tiger o'erthrown,
In a sudden shower their tears fly down.

毛泽东《蝶恋花·答李淑一》
词意图（局部）

Artistic Conception of Mao Zedong's The Immortals—Reply to Li Shuyi in the Tune "Butterflies Lingering over Flowers" (partial)

岩岭观瀑图（局部） 现代 傅抱石
Watching the Fall of Yanling Mountain (partial), Contemporary, Fu Baoshi

七 绝 · 观潮

1957 年 9 月

千里波涛滚滚来，
雪花飞向钓鱼台。
人山纷赞阵容阔，
铁马从容杀敌回。

SEVEN-CHARACTER-QUATRAIN
WATCHING THE TIDAL BORE

September 1957

Waves upon waves roll on for miles and miles;
Snowflakes on flakes fall on the fishing site.
A mountain of faces break into broad smiles;
With ease come back rows of battle steeds white.

毛泽东《七律二首·送瘟神》之一诗意图(局部) 现代 傅抱石

Artistic Conception of Mao Zedong's Poem Get Away, Pest (I) (partial), Contemporary, Fu Baoshi

七律二首·送瘟神

1958 年 7 月 1 日

其一

绿水青山枉自多,华佗无奈小虫何!
千村薜荔人遗矢,万户萧疏鬼唱歌。
坐地日行八万里,巡天遥看一千河。
牛郎欲问瘟神事,一样悲欢逐逝波。

其二

春风杨柳万千条,六亿神州尽舜尧。
红雨随心翻作浪,青山着意化为桥。
天连五岭银锄落,地动三河铁臂摇。
借问瘟君欲何往,纸船明烛照天烧。

毛泽东《七律二首·送瘟神》之二诗意图（局部） 现代 傅抱石
Artistic Conception of Mao Zedong's Poem Get Away, Pest (II) (partial), Contemporary, Fu Baoshi

Two Poems of Seven-Character-Regular-Verse
Get Away, Pest!

July 1, 1958

I

To what avail were all these streams green and hills blue?
A little germ defied the best physician's skill.
Hundreds of hamlets saw men waste where weeds o'ergrew;
Thousands of dreary homes heard vampires sing their fill.
Riding the earth, one goes eight myriad li a day;
Ranging the sky, one sees Milky Ways from afar.
If the Cowherd inquired about the Plague God, say:
"His joy is washed away just as our sorrows are."

II

The vernal wind awakens myriads of willows;
Six hundred million are masters of wisest sort.
Crimson rain, as we wish, turns into fertile billows;
Green mountains, if we will, to bridges give support.
On five sky-scraping Ridges fell our mattocks silver-bright;
O'er the land with three streams our iron arms hold sway.
May we ask the Plague God whither he would take flight?
Burn paper boats with tapers to light his skyward way!

七绝·刘蕡

1958 年

千载长天起大云,
中唐俊伟有刘蕡。
孤鸿铩羽悲鸣镝,
万马齐喑叫一声。

画云台山记图卷（局部） 现代 傅抱石
Drawing Yuntai Mountain (partial), Contemporary, Fu Baoshi

SEVEN-CHARACTER-QUATRAIN
LIU FEN
1958

A thousand years ago bright cloud rose in dark sky:
Liu Fen dared to defy eunuchs in power high.
A featherless swan hit by arrows could not fly;
All horses mute, alone a steed would voice a cry.

毛泽东《七律·到韶山》诗意图（局部） 现代 傅抱石
Artistic Conception of Mao Zedong's Poem Shaoshan Revisited (partial), Contemporary, Fu Baoshi

七律·到韶山

1959 年 6 月

别梦依稀咒逝川，故园三十二年前。
红旗卷起农奴戟，黑手高悬霸主鞭。
为有牺牲多壮志，敢教日月换新天。
喜看稻菽千重浪，遍地英雄下夕烟。

SEVEN-CHARACTER-REGULAR-VERSE
SHAOSHAN REVISITED

June 1959

I curse the bygone days which dim as dreams appear:
Thirty-two years ago when I left my home-land,
Red flags aroused the peasants to take up the spear,
While local tyrants brandished high the whip in hand.
More minds grow stronger for the martyrs' sacrifice,
Daring to move the sun and the moon to new skies.
Happy I see now wave on wave of corn and rice;
Here and there heroes come home at dusk as smokes rise.

毛泽东《七律·登庐山》诗意图(局部) 现代 傅抱石
Artistic Conception of Mao Zedong's Poem Up Mount Lu (partial), Contemporary, Fu Baoshi

七律·登庐山

1959年7月1日

一山飞峙大江边,跃上葱茏四百旋。
冷眼向洋看世界,热风吹雨洒江天。
云横九派浮黄鹤,浪下三吴起白烟。
陶令不知何处去,桃花源里可耕田?

SEVEN-CHARACTER-REGULAR-VERSE
UP MOUNT LU

July 1, 1959

A mountain stands in mid-air by the riverside;
Four hundred twists and turns lead to its crest green-dyed.
Cold looks may be cast on the world beyond the sea;
Warm winds sprinkle raindrops on mirrors of the sky.
Clouds cluster o'er nine streams where the yellow crane flies;
Waves roll down three eastern valleys whence smokes rise.
Were the poet Tao still in the Peach-Blossom Village,
Would he not find the fertile land there good for tillage?

中山陵（局部）现代 傅抱石
Sun Yat-sen's Mausoleum (partial), Contemporary, Fu Baoshi

七绝·为女民兵题照

1961年2月

飒爽英姿五尺枪，
曙光初照演兵场。
中华儿女多奇志，
不爱红装爱武装。

SEVEN-CHARACTER-QUATRAIN
MILITIA WOMEN—INSCRIPTION ON A PHOTO

February 1961

So bright and brave, with rifles five feet long,
At early dawn they shine on drilling place.
Most Chinese daughters have desire so strong
To face the powder, not powder the face.

屈原（局部） 现代 傅抱石
Qu Yuan (partial), Contemporary, Fu Baoshi

七绝·屈原

1961 年秋

屈子当年赋楚骚，
手中握有杀人刀。
艾萧太盛椒兰少，
一跃冲向万里涛。

SEVEN-CHARACTER-QUATRAIN
QU YUAN

Autumn 1961

Qu Yuan had rhymed his griefs long, long ago;
He had no sword in hand to kill the foe.
Wild weeds o'ergrown, few sweet flowers could blow;
He plunged into endless waves to end his woe.

七绝二首·纪念鲁迅八十寿辰

1961年

其一

博大胆识铁石坚，刀光剑影任翔旋。
龙华喋血不眠夜，犹制小诗赋管弦。

其二

鉴湖越台名士乡，忧忡为国痛断肠。
剑南歌接秋风吟，一例氤氲入诗囊。

Two Poems of Seven-Character-Quatrain
On the 80th Anniversary of Lu Xun's Birthday

1961

I

Broad and brave, firm as steel or stone, with deep insight,
You came into the shade or amid the swords bright.
When blood was shed at Dragon Tower on sleepless night,
You played on lute and strings to sing the martyrs' plight.

II

The southern lakeside land teemed with celebrities;
Their heart would break for national calamities.
The cavalier's wind and the heroine's autumn rain
Evaporated like cloud into poetic strain.

秋兴（局部） 现代 傅抱石
Autumn Thoughts (partial), Contemporary, Fu Baoshi

毛泽东《七律·答友人》诗意图（局部） 现代 傅抱石
Artistic Conception of Mao Zedong's Poem Reply to a Friend (partial), Contemporary, Fu Baoshi

七律·答友人

1961 年

九嶷山上白云飞，帝子乘风下翠微。
斑竹一枝千滴泪，红霞万朵百重衣。
洞庭波涌连天雪，长岛人歌动地诗。
我欲因之梦寥廓，芙蓉国里尽朝晖。

SEVEN-CHARACTER-REGULAR-VERSE
REPLY TO A FRIEND

1961

Amid sailing white clouds Nine Mysterious Peaks tower;
Riding the wind, two Queens come down from the Green Bower.
Their bamboo canes specked with a thousand tears they shed;
Their pleated dresses made of myriad clouds rose-red.
Dongting's waves surge like snow to level sky and lake;
Long Isle overflows with songs to make the earth shake.
On wings of songs I soar into the wildest dreams
To see a Lotus land bathed in morning sunbeams.

毛泽东《七绝·为李进同志题所摄庐山仙人洞照》诗意图（局部） 现代 傅抱石
Artistic Conception of Mao Zedong's Poem The Immortal's Cave (partial), Contemporary, Fu Baoshi

七绝·为李进同志题所摄庐山仙人洞照

1961 年 9 月 9 日

暮色苍茫看劲松，
乱云飞渡仍从容。
天生一个仙人洞，
无限风光在险峰。

SEVEN-CHARACTER-QUATRAIN
THE IMMORTAL'S CAVE

September 9, 1961

A sturdy pine, as viewed in twilight dim and low,
Remains at ease while riotous clouds come and go.
The Fairy Cave's a wonder wrought by Nature's hand:
The view from perilous peak is sublime and grand.

七律·和郭沫若同志

1961 年 11 月 17 日

一从大地起风雷,便有精生白骨堆。
僧是愚氓犹可训,妖为鬼蜮必成灾。
金猴奋起千钧棒,玉宇澄清万里埃。
今日欢呼孙大圣,只缘妖雾又重来。

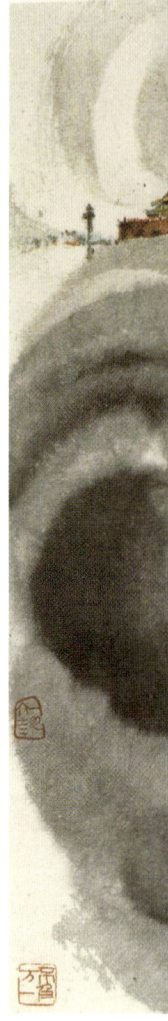

SEVEN-CHARACTER-REGULAR-VERSE
REPLY TO COMRADE GUO MORUO

November 17, 1961

With the rise of the wind-and-thunder storm on earth,
Out of white skeletons a Spirit had its birth.
The Monk might learn a lesson, though a foolish master;
The Spirit, being evil, surely brings disaster.
The Monkey swung his fabulous wand for a sweep;
The jade-like dome was cleared of all dust wide and deep.
We hail the ever-victorious Monkey King today,
For the mist-veiled Spirit is again on his way.

毛泽东《七律·和郭沫若同志》诗意图 现代 傅抱石
Artistic Conception of Mao Zedong's Poem Reply to Comrade Guo Moruo,
Contemporary, Fu Baoshi

毛泽东《卜算子·咏梅》诗意图（局部） 现代 傅抱石
Artistic Conception of Mao Zedong's Ode to the Mume Blossom in the Tune "Song Of Divination" (partial), Contemporary, Fu Baoshi

卜算子 咏梅

1961 年 12 月

风雨送春归，飞雪迎春到。
已是悬崖百丈冰，犹有花枝俏。

俏也不争春，只把春来报。
待到山花烂漫时，她在丛中笑。

TUNE: SONG OF DIVINATION
ODE TO THE MUME BLOSSOM

December 1961

Then spring departed in wind and rain;
With flying snow it's back again.
Though icicles from beetling cliffs still hang miles long,
One flower sweet and fair is there among.

Though sweet and fair, with other flowers she won't rival,
But only heralds spring's arrival.
When mountain flowers run riot for miles and miles,
Among them she will be all smiles.

七律·冬云

1962年12月26日

雪压冬云白絮飞,万花纷谢一时稀。
高天滚滚寒流急,大地微微暖气吹。
独有英雄驱虎豹,更无豪杰怕熊罴。
梅花欢喜漫天雪,冻死苍蝇未足奇。

SEVEN-CHARACTER-REGULAR-VERSE
WINTER CLOUDS

December 26, 1962

Like cotton fluff fly winter clouds hard pressed by snow;
All flowers fallen now, for a time few still blow.
In the steep sky cold waves are swiftly sweeping by;
On the vast earth warm winds gradually growing high.
Only heroes can hunt tigers and leopards down;
No brave man will be scared by wild bears black or brown.
Even mume blossoms welcome a skyful of snow;
No wonder flies are frozen to death down below.

毛泽东《七律·冬云》诗意图 现代 傅抱石
Artistic Conception of Mao Zedong's Poem Winter Clouds, Contemporary, Fu Baoshi

满江红 和郭沫若同志

1963年1月9日

小小寰球,有几个苍蝇碰壁。
嗡嗡叫,几声凄厉,几声抽泣。
蚂蚁缘槐夸大国,蚍蜉撼树谈何易。
正西风落叶下长安,飞鸣镝。

多少事,从来急;天地转,光阴迫。
一万年太久,只争朝夕。
四海翻腾云水怒,五洲震荡风雷激。
要扫除一切害人虫,全无敌。

毛泽东词意－乾坤赤（局部） 现代 傅抱石
Artistic Conception of Mao Zedong's Poetic Image Red World (partial), Contemporary, Fu Baoshi

TUNE: THE RIVER ALL RED
REPLY TO COMRADE GUO MORUO

January 9, 1963

Upon this globe so small

A few flies are running against the wall.

They hum and squeak,

With pain they shriek,

With spasms they squall.

An ant on a locust would boast 't was a big country;

A pismire could not find it easy to shake one tree.

At Chang'an the west wind is blowing off leaves dying;

Whistling arrows are flying.

Many deeds should be done

At the earliest date.

The earth turns round the sun;

For no man will time wait.

We cannot bear ten thousand years' delay.

Seize but the day!

The four seas are stirred up by angry clouds and waves;

The five continents convulsed by the storm which raves.

Sweep all vermins away,

Invincible for aye!

毛泽东词意 — 乾坤赤

Artistic Conception of Mao Zedong's Poetic Image Red World

杂言诗·八连颂

1963 年 8 月 1 日

好八连，天下传。为什么？意志坚。为人民，几十年。
拒腐蚀，永不沾。因此叫，好八连。解放军，要学习。
全军民，要自立。不怕压，不怕迫。不怕刀，不怕戟。
不怕鬼，不怕魅。不怕帝，不怕贼。奇儿女，如松柏。
上参天，傲霜雪。纪律好，如坚壁。军事好，如霹雳。
政治好，称第一。思想好，能分析。分析好，大有益。
益在哪？团结力。军民团结如一人，试看天下谁能敌。

ODE TO THE EIGHTH COMPANY

August 1, 1963

Company Eight
Known far and near.
Well known for what?
For its firm will.
Serving the people
Many a year,
Amid corruptions
Unstained still.
So it is called
Company good.

峨眉记游（局部） 现代 傅抱石
A Tour to Mount E'mei (partial), Contemporary, Fu Baoshi

Our people's army,
Learn from it you should.
All ranks and files,
Be self-reliant!
Of all oppressions
Be e'er defiant!
You should not fear
Or sword or spear!
Fear nor the ghosts
Nor the vampires,
Nor the enemy,
Nor the empires!
Ye sons are fine
Like cold-proof pine
Which pierces skies

韶山（局部） 现代 傅抱石
Shaoshan Mountain (partial), Contemporary, Fu Baoshi

And snow defies.
Well disciplined,
Firm as a wall,
You're brave and fast,
Like thunder blast,
Putting politics
First, above all,
Good at thinking,
Analyse you could.
Analysis
Will do much good.
What good at length?
Union is strength.
Army and people united as one,
We are unrivaled 'neath the sun.

长征第一山（局部） 现代 傅抱石
The First Mountain during the Long March (partial), Contemporary, Fu Baoshi

七律·吊罗荣桓同志

1963年12月

记得当年草上飞，红军队里每相违。
长征不是难堪日，战锦方为大问题。
斥鷃每闻欺大鸟，昆鸡长笑老鹰非。
君今不幸离人世，国有疑难可问谁？

SEVEN-CHARACTER-REGULAR-VERSE
ELEGY ON COMRADE LUO RONGHUAN

December 1963

I remember then our Red Army men were fleet;
We fought now here now there, so we could hardly meet.
Those days of our Long March were not too hard to bear;
Your battle of Jinzhou was decisive warfare.
A quail in bush may jeer at a high-flying roc;
An eagle sometimes flies e'en lower than a cock.
Now to our deep regret you've left this world for e'er.
With whom can I consult on knotty State affair?

晋贤图（局部） 现代 傅抱石
The Sages (partial), Contemporary, Fu Baoshi

贺新郎 读史

1964 年春

人猿相揖别。只几个石头磨过，小儿时节。

铜铁炉中翻火焰，为问何时猜得，不过几千寒热。

人世难逢开口笑，上疆场彼此弯弓月。流遍了，郊原血。

一篇读罢头飞雪，但记得斑斑点点，几行陈迹。

五帝三皇神圣事，骗了无涯过客。有多少风流人物？

盗跖庄蹻流誉后，更陈王奋起挥黄钺。歌未竟，东方白。

TUNE: CONGRATULATIONS TO THE BRIDEGROOM
READING HISTORY

Spring 1964

When man and monkey waved goodbye,

Leaving some tools of the stone age,

It was man's childish stage.

Then bronze and iron melted, flames rose high.

山阴道上（局部） 现代 傅抱石
On the Shanyin Path (partial), Contemporary, Fu Baoshi

When did man learn the art, you know?
But a few thousand years ago.
Few men exchanged broad smiles instead of blows;
They shot each other on the battlefield with bows.
The plain turned red
With blood they shed.

One book just red,
White hair snowed on my head.
I remember but a few lines,
A few traces and signs.
The sacred deeds of emperors and kings
Deceived so many people for so many springs.
How many of them deserved a real hero's name?
Rebels like Dao Zhi and Zhuang Qiao outdid their fame.
Chen Sheng revolted then
With his axe-wielding men.
Their songs ne'er ceased;
Bright was the east.

富春山色（局部）现代 傅抱石
The Mountain View along the Fuchun River (partial), Contemporary, Fu Baoshi

念奴娇 井冈山

1965 年 5 月

参天万木，千百里，飞上南天奇岳。

故地重来何所见，多了楼台亭阁。

五井碑前，黄洋界上，车子飞如跃。

江山如画，古代曾云海绿。

弹指三十八年，人间变了，似天渊翻覆。

犹记当时烽火里，九死一生如昨。

独有豪情，天际悬明月，风雷磅礴。

一声鸡唱，万怪烟消云落。

TUNE: CHARM OF A MAIDEN SINGER
MOUNT JINGGANG

May 1965

Sky-scraping trees

Extend a thousand lis

And fly up to the towering southern peak.

What have I seen when I come to seek

My old familiar places

But new pavilions and terraces?

Before the monument of the Five Wells

And formidable citadells

So steep

The carriage seems to leap.
The scenery the mountain displays
Was a blue sea in ancient days.

Thirty-eight years have gone by
In the twinkling of an eye.
The despot overthrown,
The sky was turned upside down.

江山多娇图（局部） 现代 傅抱石
Our Land Is Rich in Beauty (partial), Contemporary, Fu Baoshi

    I still remember' mid the beacon fire
    The life-and -death struggle which drew nigher and nigher.
    It seems to be but yesterday.
    Only true heroes could hold sway
    Like the bright moon hanging in the sky
    Or the thunder-storm raging on high.
    When cocks crow loud,
    All monsters disappear like smoke or cloud.

黄洋界（局部）　现代　傅抱石
Mount Jinggang (partial), Contemporary, Fu Baoshi

水调歌头 重上井冈山

1965 年 5 月

久有凌云志，重上井冈山。

千里来寻故地，旧貌变新颜。

到处莺歌燕舞，更有潺潺流水，高路入云端。

过了黄洋界，险处不须看。

风雷动，旌旗奋，是人寰。

三十八年过去，弹指一挥间。

可上九天揽月，可下五洋捉鳖，谈笑凯歌还。

世上无难事，只要肯登攀。

TUNE: PRELUDE TO THE MELODY OF WATER
MOUNT JINGGANG REASCENDED

May 1965

Above the clouds I've long aspired to soar,
And so I come up Mount Jinggang once more.
A long trip brings me to my old familiar nook,
Where everything has taken on a new look.
Here orioles sing, there swallows swirl,

O'er there streams purl,
And cloud-capped roads lead to the sky.
But after Huangyangjie,
No perilous place will arrest the eye.

The storm is raging
With flags unfurled:
Such is man's world.
Thirty-eight years are gone
As fast as a fillip is done.
We can bring down the moon from the ninth heaven,
Or catch the giant turtles in the sea,
And come back amid triumphant songs in high glee.
Nothing is hard under the sky
If we but dare to climb up high.

毛泽东《西江月·井冈山》词意图 现代 傅抱石
Artistic Conception of Mao Zedong's Mount Jinggang in the Tune "The Moon over the West River", Contemporary, Fu Baoshi

龚半千诗意图（局部） 现代 傅抱石
Poetic Image of Gong Banqian (partial), Contemporary, Fu Baoshi

念奴娇 鸟儿问答

1965 年秋

鲲鹏展翅，九万里，翻动扶摇羊角。

背负青天朝下看，都是人间城郭。

炮火连天，弹痕遍地，吓倒蓬间雀。

怎么得了，哎呀我要飞跃。

借问君去何方，雀儿答道：有仙山琼阁。

不见前年秋月朗，订了三家条约。

还有吃的，土豆烧熟了，再加牛肉。

不须放屁，试看天地翻覆。

TUNE: CHARM OF A MAIDEN SINGER
DIALOGUE BETWEEN TWO BIRDS

Autumn 1965

The roc spreads his wings and flies
Ninety thousand miles, rousing hard
Blowing cyclones. The blue skies
On his back, he looks down
And sees on earth city and town.

With gunfire the sky is loud
And by shells the earth is scarred;
The sparrow in his bush is cowed.
"What can be done? Alas the day!
I want to flit and fly away."

"May I ask where you want to go?"
And the sparrow replies,
"To a fairyland with ivory towers.
But don't you know two years ago
When the moon lit the autumn skies,
A pact was signed by three big powers?
Besides, they have for food
Potatoes cooked and beef well stewed..."
"Shut up! You bet
Heaven and earth will be upset."

山水 現代 傅抱石
Landscape, Contemporary, Fu Baoshi

唐人诗意图 现代 傅抱石

Poetic Image of the Tang Dynasty, Contemporary, Fu Baoshi

七律·洪都

1965 年

到得洪都又一年,祖生击楫至今传。
闻鸡久听南天雨,立马曾挥北地鞭。
鬓雪飞来成废料,彩云长在有新天。
年年后浪推前浪,江草江花处处鲜。

SEVEN-CHARACTER-REGULAR-VERSE
NANCHANG, CAPITAL OF JIANGXI

1965

One year has passed, again I come to Nanchang in south;
The deeds on the middlestream still spread from mouth to mouth.
We rose at cockcrow, sword in hand, in southern rain;
We reared our steeds by wielding whips on northern plain.
Useless am I now age snows on my head hair white,
But radiant clouds will ever make new heaven bright.
The waves will push each other on from year to year;
Riverside grass and flowers ever fresh will appear.

山城雄姿（局部） 现代 傅抱石

The Majestic View of a Mountainous City (partial), Contemporary, Fu Baoshi

潇潇暮雨 现代 傅抱石
A Dusk Drizzle, Contemporary, Fu Baoshi

七 律 · 有所思

1966 年 6 月

正是神都有事时，又来南国踏芳枝。

青松怒向苍天发，败叶纷随碧水驰。

一阵风雷惊世界，满街红绿走旌旗。

凭阑静听潇潇雨，故国人民有所思。

SEVEN-CHARACTER-REGULAR-VERSE YEARNING

June 1966

It's time in capital for a dream to come true;

Again I tread in southern land' mid trees in bloom.

Green pines stretch arms in wrath like bolt into the blue;

Withered leaves flow away with running waves in gloom.

A gust of stormy wind would startle men in power;

All streets are red and green with banners fluttering.

Leaning on balustrade, I listen to the shower:

My countrymen are yearning for another spring.

仿石涛山水（局部） 现代 傅抱石
An Imitation of Shi Tao's Landscape Painting (partial), Contemporary, Fu Baoshi

七 绝 · 贾谊

贾生才调世无伦，
哭泣情怀吊屈文。
梁王堕马寻常事，
何用哀伤付一生。

SEVEN-CHARACTER-QUATRAIN
JIA YI

Jia Yi the scholar had a talent without peer;
He mourned by lakeside o'er the exiled poet dear.
What had the student's death to do with the wise master?
Why should he die of grief o'er the prince's disaster?

七律·咏贾谊

少年倜傥廊庙才,壮志未酬事堪哀。
胸罗文章兵百万,胆照华国树千台。
雄英无计倾圣主,高节终竟受疑猜。
千古同惜长沙傅,空白汨罗步尘埃。

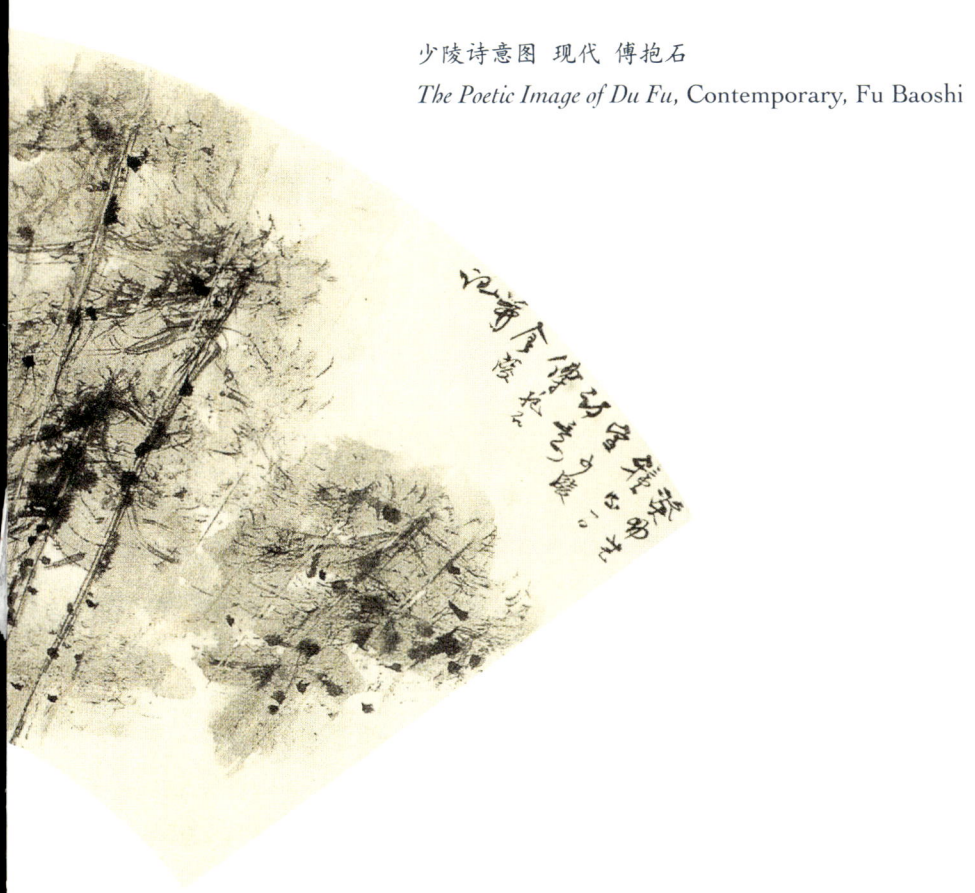

少陵诗意图 现代 傅抱石
The Poetic Image of Du Fu, Contemporary, Fu Baoshi

SEVEN-CHARACTER-REGULAR-VERSE
ON JIA YI

While young, he had the talent of serving the State;
To our regret, his ambition was not fulfilled.
He knew the way of commanding an army great,
Of strengthening the State by weakening lords self-willed.
Brave as he was, he could not persuade the king;
Loyal although he was, he fell into disgrace.
Master in Changsha, he's deplored from spring to spring.
Why should he follow, Oh! the exiled poet's trace?